40 DAY PRAYER

Praying for Someone's Salvation

Powerful day-by-day prayers, inviting God to forever change a life.

Eric Sprinkle and Laura Shaffer

Living a life
that's challenging,

ADVENTURE
EXPER✶ENCE

exhilarating and
eye-opening

TM

Adventure Experience Press
"Fanning the flame within."

Praying for Someone's Salvation: Powerful day-by-day prayers, inviting God to forever change a life.

Copyright ℗ 2021 Eric Sprinkle and Laura Shaffer

All photos by Eric Sprinkle

Cover and interior design by Robin Black

ISBN: 978-1-7322694-2-2
Published by Adventure Experience Press in partnership with the fine folks at EA Books Books Publishing, a division of Living Parables of Central Florida, Inc. a 501c3

AdventureExperience.net
EABooksPublishing.com

DEDICATIONS

Laura—To David, my husband of 45 years, whose devotion and faithfulness to me and our family has afforded me the opportunity to spend time in numerous Bible studies and prayer groups.

Eric—To my future wife. I don't know your name, don't know your face; Cutie, I don't even know where you are! But you're out there somewhere, my love, and I'm praying for you, even now.

Introduction

Let's face it, our gracious Lord God has a thing for 40 days. Forty days of rain to flood the earth, 40 days spent in the wilderness before Jesus started his ministry, 40 days before the clock ran down on Nineveh to return to Him. Over and over, we see 40 days as the time frame God uses for major changes in people and circumstances.

If I asked you to think of one person in your life that needs salvation, who immediately comes to mind? Have they ever come to mind before?

Is this the time to pray for their salvation in a way you maybe never have before?

God loves it when we talk to and share with Him through prayer. Share our thoughts, our fears, our celebrations, and concerns. The Bible tells us it's our prayers and petitions, with thanksgiving, that God uses to bring us peace (Phil 4:6-7). Jesus himself told the disciples that sometimes when casting out demons only prayer will do the trick (Mark 9:29).

Maybe it's just me, but I get the feeling that I've vastly underestimated just how powerful prayer can be—and maybe you've felt that way too?

So, let's change it up. Let's make beautiful, Bible-based, laser-focused prayers a part of our daily routine for the next 40 days. Prayers for just one person. And instead of trying to think of the words, we'll use some of the most wonderful, powerful, stirring prayers you've ever heard, from our new mutual friend, Laura.

Let's read her prayers and make them our own. Let's pray them silently or aloud, inserting the name of the person that kept coming to mind. Don't worry, that'll be almost automatic by the time you get to Day 4.

What if we add a second person to pray for? What if we invite someone else to pray with us too? What if we invite a group of friends to join us on this 40-day prayer journey? All lifting up the same person, plans and ideas to Him, asking together for the Almighty to change that person's life. To reveal Himself. To call them to Him.

Our Heavenly Father loves hearing our requests to Him through prayer. He loves blessing us with gifts too, often far more than we could ever ask or imagine.

I wonder what He wants to do in the life of that someone you know.

I say we find out.

It's time to turn the page and begin a 40-day journey, focused on the salvation of the person you've chosen, one that's most certainly going to impact them, and you as well.

Are you ready?

Let's do this.

Acknowledgements

- Thank-you to the Team at **EA Books** for all the help!
- **Cover Artist Robin**—for making the book look good—truly good—inside and out.
- **Editor Amy**—thank you for making it an enlightening, fun, and painless process as always.
- To Laura's Facebook peeps who responded quickly with such wonderful and specific feedback.
- Laura also thanks her amazing prayer partners who taught her so much about how to pray and how to listen for God's answers by example, over the years from Bible studies, Moms in Prayer, Torah group, and our Community Group. Extra special thanks go to Cathy and Michelle—prayer partners who prayed with me through the "40 Days—Salvation" prayers. Their support and suggestions were invaluable.
- Eric also thanks Panera Bread, Colorado Springs for a place to come and lay his laptop, all throughout Covid.
- Lastly and always, to our Gracious Lord God, who hears and is moved to act by our prayers.

Soli Deo Gloria.

How to use the 40-Day Prayer Guide

Prayer pages:

The guide will give you one area of salvation to pray each day for 40 days.

You can simply pray the prayer as it is, with the name of your person _____ in the blanks, or you can let the Holy Spirit guide you and use your own words.

There may be times when a particular problem or situation in the life of the person you're praying for will take precedence over a pre-planned agenda of prayer. That's ok.

Being flexible and sensitive to the Holy Spirit is the most important thing. Simply being intentional and consistent in your prayer time will help you be sensitive to the Holy Spirit.

Reflections pages:

Every seven days the guide will give you opportunities to:

• Write down your thoughts as you go along.
• Evaluate your progress.
• Look for ways God may be answering your prayers and thank Him.
• See how He is speaking to you personally about your prayer life, or how God might be leading you in your life.

There are, of course, many things you can ask for as you pray to bring your person to a saving relationship to Jesus Christ. This is not meant to list or speak to all of them.

It will, however, help you be more intentional and consistent in praying. And by spending time in prayer, you will be open to the Spirit's leading. Learning to listen to the Holy Spirit guide you is most important.

It is our prayer that you will grow in your prayer life as you pray for _____. That this person will benefit for eternity from the answers to your prayers.

And that you will be blessed as you *lean in and learn* from the Lord through prayer.

Before Beginning

Reflections page...

Are you willing to set aside a few minutes each day to pray aloud for _____ to come to know Jesus Christ as their Savior?

It may help to imagine a specific and regular time of day or place to be sure you are being intentional and consistent in your praying (like when you first get up, or while exercising, driving to work, or during a break from work, or in a room or seat in your home at a certain time, or at a natural break in your routine).

When praying for another person, also called interceding in prayer, or intercession, there is wisdom in preparing yourself as well. Two areas are important:

1—Confession and Repentance—The Bible tells us in Psalm 66:18, "If I had cherished sin in my heart, the Lord would not have listened." It is important to take time to ask God to search your heart and show you any sin you need to confess and repent of before you move into interceding for _____.

God has promised that *"If we confess our sins, he is faithful and just and will forgive us our sins and purify us from all unrighteousness"* (1 John 1:9).

2—Arm for Battle—Ephesians tells us to be *"strong in the Lord and in His mighty power. Put on the full armor of God"* (6:10-11). So, we need to do that.

If either of these are new to you, there's some instruction in the Appendix at the back of this book on pages 109-113.

Prayer Tips

Are all prayers equal? It seems that God has listed some guidelines for us in Scripture that can either compromise or boost the effectiveness of our prayers.

There are even things that can cause Him to choose to step back and even disregard our prayers for a time. Yikes! Others are just the opposite, creating a multiplying effect on our prayers.

Have a look through and make sure nothing listed is going to get in your way over the next 40 days.

Some Biblical Guidelines

"The prayer of a righteous person is powerful and effective" (James 5:16).

Be sure you're following God and steering away from anything unrighteous or purposefully against God's ways for living. Holding grudges, being angry, indulging in wrongful thoughts or actions can all take away from the effectiveness of your 40-day journey.

"The eyes of the LORD are on the righteous, and his ears are attentive to their cry" (Psalm 34:15).

Exactly the opposite, we can rest assured we have God's complete attention when pursuing right living in our actions and choices.

"Then Jesus told his disciples a parable to show them that they should always pray and not give up" (Luke 18:1).

No worries there, you're going to be praying for the next 40 days, so you've got this!

"When you ask you do not receive, because you ask with wrong motives, that you may spend what you get on your pleasures" (James 4:3).

Okay, so praying for your boss to be saved just so you get a promotion is not allowed, agreed?

"But your iniquities have separated you from your God; your sins have hidden his face from you, so that he will not hear" (Isaiah 59:2).

Again, let's be careful we don't have sin in our hearts that will get in the way of what we're asking. If we want to see the stars, let's get away from light pollution. If we want to talk to God, let's clear out the background noise and use a strong signal with four bars.

"This is the confidence we have in approaching God: that if we ask anything according to his will, he hears us" (1 John 5:14).

Let's all be sure we're asking for things in line with His will, His plans, His timing, and not our own. Trust that God is actively working to draw this person to Him, for His Glory, even if we're not seeing anything happening right away.

Additional ideas that can boost the impact of your praying

- Pray these prayers out loud.

   Does it help God hear them better? No. Does it help you? You bet! Praying out loud helps you slow down and focus on the person and words you're praying - allowing time for the Holy Spirit to meet you in your prayer. And that can make a difference all on its own.

- As the Holy Spirit brings additional things to mind when you're praying, pray those too.

- Pray the daily prayer multiple times each day.

   Anytime you eat? Morning and Evening? Or maybe whenever you start your car?

- Pray for more than one person.

   What happens if you say two people's names for each prayer?

- Pray this 40 Day journey with a friend.

   Both of you, lifting the same person in prayer.

- Consider fasting at some point during the journey.

   Giving up TV, social media, or even certain foods for a week during your journey will only serve to sharpen your spiritual focus!

Don't miss the Appendix Resources

Quick, the person you're praying for is on the phone, admitting they're done; they want to surrender. To join Team Jesus. And suddenly, they're asking you how to receive Christ!

I love it! But now what do you do?!?

No worries. Check out our Appendix at the back of this book for valuable resources you might need during your 40 day Journey. Whether that's how to specifically "armor up," explaining words like "repent," fielding questions related to salvation, or even a step-by-step Salvation Prayer, you're covered.

Table of Contents

Show Them You Care (Help them realize God's love is for them, as is Salvation)

PART 1

Prepare Them

My Commitment

For this reason I kneel before the Father... I pray that out of his glorious riches he may strengthen you with power through his Spirit in your inner being, so that Christ may dwell in your hearts through faith (Ephesians 3:14, 16-17).

In the power of the name of the Lord Jesus Christ, I am offering these prayers. Father, I am trusting You to act and effect Your will during these next 40 days of prayer for _____, to bring them to salvation through the shed blood and resurrection of Jesus Christ my Lord and Savior.

Father, I cannot even imagine all the forces that are currently influencing _____'s life. I know that the devil and the world and even our own flesh are at war with You and what is holy. Those forces seek to keep people away from You and the truth. And entice _____ into attitudes and behaviors that are harmful and doom them to spend eternity apart from You. Please be at work in _____'s life in ways that only You can.

Especially during these 40 days of prayer, be their strength and spread Your protection over _____'s body, mind and spirit. Watch over their physical health so no illness sidelines them. Meet their emotional needs where relationships have been broken by betrayal, unmet expectations, or dishonesty. Heal any spiritual wounds where they have been believing lies that kept them away from Your perfect love and salvation. Thank You for being their Healer: Jehovah Rophe.

As for me, I will put on Your spiritual armor every day for these 40 days (Ephesians 6:10-17). And I will stand in the gap for _____ (Ezekiel 22:30). I will intercede for their salvation, asking that You will contend with those who contend with them and fight against those who fight against them to give them victory over the enemies of their soul (Psalm 35:1).

I humbly ask for Your will to be done in and through _____'s life. Father, prepare them for the message of salvation. Make them aware that they need Your salvation, and show them that You care, always. Amen

2

Dispel the Darkness

For he has rescued us from the dominion of darkness and brought us into the kingdom of the Son he loves, in whom we have redemption, the forgiveness of sins (Colossians 1:13-14).

Heavenly Father, please do all in Your power to dispel the darkness _____ is living in now. Overcome the lies and deceitful thoughts that have been allowed into their mind and heart. Open _____'s eyes to the truth—about You, about Your love for them, about their need for a Savior in Jesus Christ. Show the harm _____ is causing their body and their mind and soul and spirit, and about the real source of these lies, misinformation and deceiving thoughts _____ has allowed themselves to live and be led by.

Father I am asking that right now, for these 40 days, You would place people around _____ who will be witnesses to them of the hope and truth and light that is in Christ Jesus. Break through whatever is keeping _____ in dark moods or downcast emotional states. Allow _____ to feel the love once again You have for them.

Thank You for saving _____'s physical life. Thank You for intervening in the plans of the evil one who comes to harm, kill, and destroy. Please continue to fight for _____ and guard that life. Breathe Your love and encouragement into _____ to deliver them from the darkness that seeks to overwhelm and destroy them. Give _____ a hope and a resolve to turn from the darkness to Your light.

Lord, change _____'s very life. You are a God of unlimited power and can do immeasurably more than I can ask or even imagine (Ephesians 3:20). Let _____ be the recipient of Your amazing love and transforming power and be a living testimony to the lengths You will go to, to save one of Your own precious lambs. Father, honor our prayers for this precious lamb. Amen

Heart of Stone to Heart of Flesh

I will give you a new heart and put a new spirit in you; I will remove from you your heart of stone and give you a heart of flesh (Ezekiel 36:26).

Heavenly Father, You have said it is Your will for none to perish but that everyone come to a saving knowledge and relationship with You (2 Peter 3:9). I am praying in alignment with Your desire for _____ to know of Your love for them. And for them to realize how You sent Your son Jesus to live on this earth and die on the cross, shedding His blood to pay the price of our sin in order to restore a personal and right relationship with You.

Father, in the Old Testament there was a prophecy that when You came again You would *"remove [their] heart of stone and give [them] a heart of flesh"* (Ezekiel 36:26). I pray for _____ now, that You would remove their heart of stone and whatever has made them so hard, and give them a heart of flesh to bring them to salvation.

Father may that new heart be softened and open to understanding Your love for them. May it show _____ Your provision for them to come to You, confess, and receive forgiveness for their sins which You so freely offer. Prepare their heart to be opened to receive the Holy Spirit and know Jesus Christ as Savior, securing their position as Your child to spend eternity with You. Amen

Question Their Beliefs

[Jesus speaking] I am sending you to them to open their eyes and turn them from darkness to light, and from the power of Satan to God, so that they may receive forgiveness of sins and a place among those who are sanctified by faith in me (Acts 26:17-19).

Heavenly Father I am trusting you to prepare the heart and mind of _____ who does not know You. Cause them to question their belief system, whatever it is that they have put their confidence and their trust in as a means of organizing and living their life and making decisions.

Pull back the veil of lies and deceit _____ has believed, that have come from either the world with its philosophies and marketing strategies that lead people away from living humble and contented lives, or through the evil one who roams around like a lion looking for someone to devour, 1 Peter 5:8. Rip away the evil one's trickery and schemes that have drawn them away from You. Help them see that You alone can redeem them.

Show _____ where they have trusted the logic of the mind to think their way to the wrong conclusion. Or believed something not because it's true but because they admire the person who said it or because they wanted to fit in with others. Father, these beliefs deceive them into believing lies about the truth of a successful and fulfilled life. As _____ makes decisions, shine a light on anything false so they can see it for what it is and reject it to seek the truth.

Tear down any strongholds they have built in their mind and in their life as a way of bolstering the way they have chosen to make decisions and live their life. Cause them to have a thirst for the truth and direct their path in seeking the truth. Remove any obstacles that come between them and Your truth of salvation.

Spoil the plans and the snares that the evil one sets to keep _____ trapped in darkness and deception. Contend with those who contend with _____. Fight against those who fight against You and who seek to harm, kill, and destroy _____ (Psalm 35:1). Amen

*The heavens declare the
glory of God; the skies proclaim
the work of his hands. Day after day
they pour forth speech; night after night
they reveal knowledge.*

Psalm 19:1-2

Bring Spiritual Issues to Light

Heavenly Father, I pray that You will use Your vast resources to bring spiritual issues to light in _____'s life. They will not attend church services, or pick up a Bible, so use the everyday things in their life to bring spiritual issues to the forefront of their mind.

If _____ sees a beautiful sunrise or sunset, draw their thoughts not to just the beauty they see with their eyes, but also to the One who created the sun, the earth, the stars, and their eyes to see the wonderful creation. If they look at the stars at night, let them marvel at the One who put them there and spoke the universe into creation.

As they see people dealing with problems or wrestling with questions, let them see who they go to for help and encouragement. And observe whether help comes. If _____ hears of someone who is very ill or dying, let them ponder their own mortality and where they will spend eternity. Use holidays, seasons, and current events to draw their attention to You.

Even if someone sneezes and they hear the words "bless you" let the meaning of a true blessing rise into their consciousness. Father, use daily occurrences to draw _____'s thoughts to spiritual truths to make even the mundane holy. And let those realizations sink deep into their thoughts and begin to affect their reality.

As _____ sees people enjoy what they would call good luck, let them make the connection that it is You who bless and give good gifts. Open their minds and thoughts to the truth of Your love for them and desire to be in close relationship with them. Amen

Lay Them on the Altar

Then God said, "Take your son, your only son, whom you love—Isaac—and go to the region of Moriah. Sacrifice him there as a burnt offering on a mountain I will show you" (Genesis 22:2).

Heavenly Father, I admit that no matter how deeply I want _____ to experience salvation from You, I cannot make it happen. Only You call. And only You save.

_____ is Yours! Your creation. Your child. And You know better than I do what they need and how to help them find their way to You. I cannot heal them or save them. Sometimes I cannot even help them. Yet my heart breaks over their pain.

Lord, please reach out to _____ in a way that they understand and connect to You. And reward even the tiniest baby steps they take in Your direction. Help _____ surrender whatever they need to lay aside to be in close fellowship with You. Help them tear down the walls they have constructed that keep them away from You. And Father, would You, in Your might and power, tear down any strongholds the evil one has built in their lives.

Remove the blinders that keep them believing lies and living in darkness. Just as the stars shine bright in the sky, shine brightly in their life and heart and spirit, and dispel the darkness around them—whatever the source.

Heavenly Father just as You commanded Abraham to lay Isaac on the sacrificial altar, I acknowledge that _____ is your child. And that even though they mean the world to me, I lay _____ on the altar as a sacrifice to say that I acknowledge I am not in control of their life or even the factors that affect their attitudes or decision-making process. I surrender whatever hold or control I thought I had over them and I leave them in Your capable and loving hands.

I give You the thanks and praise in advance for how You will work in their lives, I wait, anticipating Your deliverance. Amen

Use Other Christians

Do not be misled, "Bad company corrupts good character" (1 Corinthians 15:33).

Heavenly Father, I ask that You bring Christians into _____'s life who will be able to act as godly role models and mentors to _____. These don't have to be perfect people. But _____ has been put off by Christians and hypocrisy in the past, so let these people be more the way You describe in Proverbs 27:17, *"as iron sharpens iron, so one person sharpens another."* And not iron poking iron.

Let these believers have a positive influence on _____ and give wise counsel when they must make a decision or consider an issue of the day. Let these people share a godly perspective on the world and what's happening around them.

Let _____ see how these believers are in the world but not of the world. Let _____ see how their language, demeanor, attitudes, and actions show Your love to those around them.

As I am a believer too, lead me in how to love _____ with Your love. Guard my mouth so I do not speak in a condemning, confusing, or counterproductive manner. And give me the wisdom to know when to speak and when to keep quiet. Give me the patience I need to continue to show Your love to them even if I don't feel like it. And prompt me when to take an action that will benefit _____'s understanding of salvation.

Help me be an example of godliness in _____'s life. And show me how to love them best, and in doing so, show Your love for them. Amen

Reflections

If you have been able to be consistent in praying this week—good for you!

If not, what has gotten in your way?

_____

_____

_____

How can you remedy that?

_____

_____

_____

If you have missed any days, begin now from the last day you were consistent.

_____

_____

_____

During your prayer time, has God showed you anything this week about Himself? About the one you're praying for.? About yourself?

_____

_____

_____

In thinking back over the prayers prayed this week...

Is there a specific darkness you see in _____'s life to pray through?

_____

_____

_____

Are there specific beliefs they need to overcome that stand in the way of believing in Jesus Christ?

_____

_____

_____

How hard is it to lay _____ on the altar and walk away? What is hard for you to give up in their life?

_____

_____

_____

Ask God to help you be willing to give Him control of their life, decisions, influences. That may mean holding your tongue when you want to give your opinion.

_____

_____

_____

Recognition of Sin

For all have sinned and fall short of the glory of God
(Romans 3:23).

For the wages of sin is death; but the gift of God is eternal life.
In Christ Jesus our Lord (Romans 6:23).

Heavenly Father, there is a kind of law of human nature that crosses cultures whereby people know the difference between right and wrong. We don't like to be wrong and will make excuses for our actions or behavior to try to escape punishment, ridicule, or rejection. But the truth is we all make wrong choices. We all sin. You define sin as missing the mark, and the mark is perfection.

In the Old Testament you give us Ten Commandments. Because there is no human capable of living a sin-free life, You sent Your son Jesus to the earth within the frailties of humanity. He was the only one—both human and God—who was able to live a sin-free life.

Because there is a price to pay for sin, it is important for _____ to realize that all human beings sin. Every one of us. I have sinned. _____ has sinned. Breaking even one small part of Your Law is being guilty of breaking the whole of it. And the price of that sin is eternal separation from You.

But You have paid that price and offer it to _____ freely. Help them make the connection that they need You for Salvation because of their sin.

Open _____'s eyes and heart to see the specific sins they need to confess, turn away from, and ask forgiveness for. Lead _____ to see their sin for what it is. Maybe for the first time. And let it draw them to You. Amen

The god of this age has blinded the minds of the unbelievers, to keep them from seeing the light of the gospel of the glory of Christ, who is the image of God

2 Corinthians 4:4

Clear Vision

Heavenly Father, I ask that You open _____'s eyes to see the world as it really is. Remove the blinders the evil one has placed over their eyes. Grant _____ clear vision of not only what they see around them in this amazing physical world You have made, but also of the circumstances in their life.

Let _____ see the truth of what their future holds in the direction they're headed without You. Let them see spiritually what is happening around them. Give _____ a supernatural ability to understand spiritual things. Open their eyes to the reality of what thoughts and misconceptions go into making their decisions and affecting their behavior.

And show _____ what their life can look like when they put their trust in You. Build _____'s faith so that regardless of what may happen and how things look, they will be encouraged to keep moving forward toward You. Amen

Past Hurts

Heal me, Lord, and I will be healed; save me and I will be saved, for you are the one I praise (Jeremiah 17:14).

Heavenly Father, there are so many things that happen to people in their life that cause pain: physical, psychological, mental, and emotional. Some things are accidents or misunderstandings, and others are through the evil intentions of another person.

Sometimes these hurts make people bitter against You and they build a wall to keep You away without realizing that You are the only one who can bring true healing into their life. Father, whatever has happened to _____ in their life, would You bring healing to those memories, those circumstances. Would You begin to tear down the wall _____ has built up to keep You out of their life, thinking they are making themselves safer and protected.

Please provide whatever _____ needs: counseling, a friend, a role model, mentor, someone to lean on who will not judge them or lead them into the solutions that the world offers. Your Word says, *"Heal me, Lord, and I will be healed"* (Jeremiah 17:14). I'm asking you to heal _____ physically, psychologically, mentally, emotionally, and spiritually. And to get rid of any bitterness that causes them to keep You at a distance.

It may take time but begin the healing process so they can see Your light shining through whatever darkness they've been walking through. Amen

Psalm 35

For our struggle is not against flesh and blood, but against the rulers, against the authorities, against the powers of this dark world and against the spiritual forces of evil in the heavenly realms (Ephesians 6:12).

Heavenly Father, I know that beyond the circumstances of _____'s life and the attitudes and hurts from their past they hold against You, there are also spiritual enemies who fight to keep _____ away from You and an understanding of salvation. So, I put their name into Psalm 35 and pray Your words against the rulers, against the authorities, and against the spiritual powers of this dark world, and the spiritual forces in the heavenly realms who set themselves up against You and Your will for _____ (Ephesians 6:12).

Psalm 35 Of David

Contend, LORD, with those who contend with [_____];
   fight against those who fight against [them].
Take up shield and armor;
   arise and come to [their] aid.
Brandish spear and javelin
   against those who pursue [_____].
Say to [_____],
   "I am your salvation."
May those who seek [_____'s] life
   be disgraced and put to shame;
may those who plot [their] ruin
   be turned back in dismay.
May they be like chaff before the wind,
   with the angel of the LORD driving them away;
may their path be dark and slippery,
   with the angel of the Lord pursuing them.

Since they hid their net for [_____] without cause
    and without cause dug a pit for [them],
may ruin overtake them by surprise
    may the net they hid entangle them,
    may they fall into the pit, to their ruin.
Then my soul will rejoice in the LORD
    and delight in his salvation.
My whole being will exclaim,
    "Who is like you, LORD?
You rescue the poor [_____] from those too strong for them,
    the poor and needy [_____] from those who rob them."

Ruthless witnesses come forward;
    they question [_____] on things [they] know nothing about.
They repay [_____] evil for good
    and leave [them] like one bereaved.
But when [_____] stumbled, they gathered in glee;
    assailants gathered against [_____] without [their] knowledge.
    They slandered [them] without ceasing.
Like the ungodly they maliciously mocked;
    they gnashed their teeth at [_____].

How long, Lord, will you look on?
    Rescue [_____] from their ravages,
    [their] precious life from these lions.
I will give you thanks in the great assembly;
    among the throngs I will praise you.
Do not let those gloat over [_____]
    who are [their] enemies without cause;
do not let those who hate [_____] without reason
    maliciously wink the eye.
They do not speak peaceably,
    but devise false accusations
    against those who live quietly in the land.
They sneer at [_____] and say, "Aha! Aha!
    With our own eyes we have seen it."

LORD, you have seen this; do not be silent.
  Do not be far from [_____], Lord.
Awake, and rise to [_____'s] defense!
  Contend for [them], my God and Lord.
Vindicate [_____] in your righteousness, LORD MY GOD;
  do not let them gloat over [_____].
Do not let them think, "Aha, just what we wanted!"
  or say, "We have swallowed [them] up."

May all who gloat over [_____'s] distress
  be put to shame and confusion;
may all who exalt themselves over [_____]
  be clothed with shame and disgrace.
May those who delight in [_____'s] vindication
  shout for joy and gladness;
may they always say, "The LORD be exalted,
  who delights in the well-being of his servant."

My tongue will proclaim Your righteousness,
  Your praises all day long.

Amen

But if you do not forgive others their sins,
your Father will not forgive your sins.

Matthew 6:15

Forgiveness (from the Steps to Freedom in Christ)

But if you do not forgive others their sins, your Father will not forgive your sins (Matthew 6:15).

Heavenly Father, help _____ to forgive. I don't know all of them, but You know the people they haven't forgiven. Bring something into _____'s life today that shows them the importance of forgiveness and who they need to forgive. I thank You that You are a God of forgiveness, patience, and kindness. Thank You that You not only forgive our sin, but that You paid the penalty our sins deserve with Your blood on the cross.

Help _____ release any bitterness and resentment they have or are harboring against those who have offended them and extend that same forgiveness. Sometimes that hardest person to forgive is oneself, so show _____ where they need to forgive themself.

Often people think they must clean up their act before coming to You. Let _____ know that You stand ready to forgive them and welcome them with open arms. Rather than sinking into self-punishing behaviors for their wrong choices and sins, let _____ accept the truth that You forgive them through Jesus Christ.

Father, let _____ even let go of anger against You for anything they believe You may have done or failed to do in their life. Help them fully express that to You and let go of any resentment. Heal their emotions and bless _____ as they walk in the victory of forgiveness. Amen

Dreams and Visions

I will pour out my Spirit on all people. Your sons and daughters will prophesy, your young men will see visions, your old men will dream dreams (Joel 2:28).

Heavenly Father, You are at work at all times and in every place around the world, and in the life of every person. Even those people without a translation of the Bible have access to You as You reach them with dreams and visions of who You are. And of Your love for them.

Would you give _____ a dream or vision? Whether it's a dream or vision of future events, or a revelation that You are the Savior of mankind and of the power that You possess as Creator of this universe. Reach their mind and heart and spirit with Your truth that even as Almighty God, You love _____ and desire to have a saving relationship with them.

I have heard of nonbelievers in foreign countries, with governments who suppress Your truth, having literal dreams while they sleep, where You revealed Yourself as Savior. And when they wake up the truth remains with them. I have heard of people having sleeping dreams about where their life is headed without You and they wake up with the realization that they need a change: You in their life! Father, wake up _____ with a realization of who You are.

I have heard of people who have had experiences that caused them to have a flash or a waking vision that has figuratively woken them up to the reality that they have been living their life focused on the wrong goals. And they completely turn their lives around and give themselves to You. Father, get _____'s attention with an experience or revelation they can't deny.

Would You cause this kind of change in _____? Reach them in a way that I cannot. In a way that only You can. Change the course of their life by drawing them to You in a way that captures their attention and their imagination. Amen

Keep From Evil

Blessed is the one who does not walk in step with the wicked or stand in the way that sinners take or sit in the company of mockers (Psalm 1:1).

F ather do not let _____ mock You with their words, their actions, or their attitudes. And don't let them follow the example of other people who do. Do not let them take Your name in vain or deny Your presence or Your work here on earth. Stop _____ from following the crowd and participating in activities that expose them to wickedness.

Father protect them and guide them in their comings and goings. Do not let _____ seek after evil or be tempted by the temporary pleasures of evil. But let them see what is good and right and just. Let them have experiences that bear out Your truth about what is overtly evil and what is good. Even let _____ learn from the painful lessons and experiences of others that evil does not pay, and that it will cost them more than they anticipate.

Instead, let _____ feel the love You have for them and the care You have taken of them. If they are around evil, let them feel uncomfortable and run from those people or activities or places, literally and figuratively. If they stumble upon evil, open their eyes to see the harm and the trap before they get drawn into it.

Wherever _____ is spiritually, let them sense You watching over them and remember that they are Yours. And let that be a powerful deterrent, and an awesome reassurance. Amen

Reflections

If you have been able to be consistent in praying this week—good for you!

If not, what has gotten in your way?
How can you remedy that?

_____

_____

_____

If you have missed any days, go back, and pray any prayers you missed. Take extra days if you need to.

_____

_____

_____

During your prayer time, has God showed you anything this week about Himself? About the one you're praying for?

_____

_____

_____

About yourself?

_____

_____

_____

In thinking back over the prayers prayed this week...

Have you ever had a dream or vision from God—in a general or a specific sense?

_____

_____

_____

Have you shared it with anyone? What was the reaction?

_____

_____

_____

Are you aware of any specific evil influences in _____'s life to pray against?

_____

_____

_____

PART 2

Make Them Aware

See the Creator

Do you not know? Have you not heard? The Lord is the everlasting God, the Creator of the ends of the earth (Isaiah 40:28).

Heavenly Father, so many people marvel and wonder at the amazing world we live in—the intricate details of how a human eye works, the wide variety of insect species, or the number of factors that must be held in balance for life to exist on earth. But they stop there and chalk it up to coincidence, happenstance, or big bang theory, and don't look past that. Give _____ the ability to look beyond the miraculous to the miracle worker behind it all. To see past the creation to the Creator!

No one would marvel at a building, its design, magnitude, structure, or beauty, without acknowledging there was an architect. No one would appreciate a painting with its colors, form, or content, without crediting the artist. So why is it that something infinitely more complex, like the human body or the universe is explained away without giving credit to its Creator?

Father, help _____ see past what is right in front of them to the imagination, the endless creativity, the complexity, diversity, power, and sovereignty only You possess to bring all this into being...and keep it going!

You tell us that the recognition and glory are due the Creator. Impress on _____ to acknowledge Your handiwork and make room in their life to respect You, the Creator, their Creator, THE Creator. Amen

Believe the Bible is True

All Scripture is God-breathed and is useful for teaching, rebuking, correcting, and training in righteousness (2 Timothy 3:16).

Then you will know the truth and the truth will set you free (John 8:32).

Heavenly Father, open _____'s eyes and mind to accept that Jesus is more than a historic figure who lived and died in Israel 2000 years ago. Give them the ability to comprehend that Jesus was the actual, living, Son of God who came to earth as a baby and lived a sinless life. And that there was purpose in His death, beyond the historic events of it.

Lead _____ to an awareness and understanding in their head, in their heart, and in their spirit of who You are and of Your great love for them to have made the unimaginable sacrifice on the cross. Help them believe the words they read and have heard about the meaning of that sacrifice for their life. And lead them into the acceptance of that free gift.

Establish in _____'s mind and understanding that the Bible is more than a collection of nice stories. And that it has been the number one most published and read book of all time because it teaches the truth about the world and the One True God.

Heavenly Father, let Your Word be implanted into good soil in _____. And reap a harvest of victory in their salvation! Amen.

Sense Your Presence

You make known to me the path of life; you will fill me with joy in your presence, with eternal pleasures at your right hand (Psalm 16:11).

Heavenly Father, open _____'s awareness to be able to sense Your presence with them. Let _____ feel You in real and tangible ways.
Father, You know best what _____ needs. Meet a need in a way that they know without a doubt that it came from You. If _____ needs encouragement, send someone with an encouraging word or note or expression of appreciation. If having a problem, show them a creative and unique solution they never could have thought of. Whether it's a phone call from a friend at the right time, the perfect parking place, or a smile from a stranger, reveal that it is a gift from You.

Or maybe Your presence is simply the feeling of calm and peace amidst challenging circumstances. Let Your presence be an awesome reassurance of security that _____ can enjoy through a difficulty.

Some of us feel closer to You when we are in nature, like taking a walk or a hike. Or watching a sunset. Or listening to a stream. Or seeing birds fly overhead. Father give _____ that sense that they are not alone and that there is something much larger, more powerful, and creative, and good at work in the world and in their life.

For some it's meditating, being quiet and reaching out to connect with some power outside themself. Father, if _____ reaches out, let them connect with You.

Maybe it will be through music, or in helping others, or some physical activity...however _____ may search, protect that search so they find You. Don't let them be fooled or enticed or misled by any other power. Amen

Pride vs Humility

But he gives us more grace. That is why Scripture says: "God opposes the proud but shows favor to the humble." Submit yourselves, then, to God. Resist the devil, and he will flee from you...Humble yourselves before the Lord, and he will lift you up (James 4:6 -7, 10).

Heavenly Father, You tell us You oppose the proud but give grace to the humble. In this world we often seek to be good at things so others will respect and admire us. We want to be worthy of other people's respect and admiration. Pride is even a way we have learned to protect ourselves from the harshness of others.

But it also creates a wall of arrogance that keeps us from You. Father, cut through _____'s prideful attitude that keeps them believing they are self-sufficient and don't need You in their life. Help them see humility as a worthy attitude. And be willing to see You as an authority in their life. Teach _____ that submission is not a bad thing, but a way of using their power under control, under Your authority.

Show _____ how to use their power to resist the devil and submit it to Your authority and protection. And how by doing that, the devil will flee from them because when seen under Your authority, the devil is no match for You.

Show _____ how to draw near to You—through prayer, Your Word, worship music, praise, and fellowship with other believers. And that when that happens, it is You who come near and lift those who have humbled themselves. Amen

Send Evangelists

How beautiful on the mountains are the feet of those who bring good news, who proclaim peace, who bring good tidings, who proclaim salvation, who say to Zion, "Your God reigns!" (Isaiah 52:7)

Heavenly Father, please send evangelists into _____'s life. People who will speak the message of the Good News in a clear and persuasive way. People who are anointed to share without being judgmental or overbearing. Father, let _____ be exposed to Your offer of salvation in a way that is palatable for them and at a time when You have prepared them to hear it and understand it.

When _____ hears Your message calling them personally, let those words sink deep into their spirit. And let it stir in _____ an awareness of what they have been missing, what they've been looking for, to have a purposeful and joyous life.

You say Your word does not return empty but will accomplish all You desire and achieve the purpose for which You send it out, Isaiah 55:10-11. So let the message of Your salvation fill _____ and achieve the purpose of their salvation.

Father, in addition to the evangelists You send _____ now, I pray that You would activate their memory to recall Your Word, Your message that has been implanted in them all throughout their life. Recall to their mind sermons they have heard, scripture they have memorized, Bible stories they have known. Let them remember Christian worship songs they sang and even prayers they have prayed or have been prayed over them.

Use all these experiences from their past to bring them to the awareness that they need You now in their present and for their eternal future. Father, bring Your message of salvation to bear on them now in a way that makes a difference in eternity. I rejoice over Your Good News. And I rejoice in advance of _____'s acceptance of that Good News also. Amen

DAY 20

Stop Victim Mentality

"They will fight against you but will not overcome you, for I am with you and will rescue you," declares the Lord (Jeremiah 1:19).

For the Spirit God gave us does not make us timid, but gives us power, love and self-discipline (2 Timothy 1:7).

Heavenly Father regardless of what has happened in _____'s life I pray that You would help them stop seeing themselves as a victim. At some point, either because of the evil and abuse of other people or refusing to accept responsibility for their own actions, _____ has chosen to see themself as a victim. It has robbed them of their ability to make wise decisions and take charge of their life.

The victim mentality has brought some benefit in their life and has won them petty attention from others. But it will ultimately blind them to see their need for a savior and receive Your love and the salvation You offer. Father, do not let _____ choose the benefit of being a victim over a victory with You.

Seeing themself as a victim allows _____ to complain, rebel, blame others, wallow in self-pity, and feel like they have nothing to do but lay down and die. But if _____ were simply just to see themself as an overcomer and accept Your love, they would be empowered to pray, to believe in Your ability to work in their life, and to move forward no matter their circumstances or past experiences.

Father You have given us authority to overcome all the power of the enemy, (Luke 10:19). Help _____ lay down their victim mentality and take up the mantle of "Overcomer." As they do that, show them Your love in a way they can understand and sense in a real and tangible way, and acknowledge that You are the Savior they have always needed. Amen.

Divine Appointments

"For I know the plans I have for you," declares the Lord, "plans to prosper you and not to harm you, plans to give you a hope and a future" (Jeremiah 29:11).

Heavenly Father, give _____ "Divine Appointments" in their life. Arrange opportunities for them to be in the right place at the right time to hear or see something or someone who will contribute to their understanding of Your love for them, and Your provision for their life.

Orchestrate meetings with other people who can introduce them to the beauty of a life lived for You. Lead them to people who exemplify godly behavior, language, and motivation.

Whether these will become lifelong friendships, or just be a momentary influence in their life, let these happenings occur often. Let them create a constant stream of positive, godly, and encouraging direction for _____.

Let them witness events or casual occurrences that make a connection with You and Your power. You created the universe! Help them discover You in a podcast, or in the theme of a movie or in a real-life discussion, joy or challenge. When these divine appointments happen, don't let _____ miss the significance of what is occurring. Open their mind and heart and spirit to the influences You bring their way. Amen

Reflections

You are more than halfway through this 40-day journey!
Great job!!

If you have not been able to be consistent in praying this week,
what has gotten in your way?

_____

_____

_____

How can you remedy that?

_____

_____

If you have missed any days, go back, and pray any prayers you
missed. Take extra days if you need to.

During your prayer time, has God showed you anything this week
about Himself? About the one you're praying for?
About yourself?

_____

_____

_____

In thinking back over the prayers prayed this week...

How old were you when you started reading the Bible?

_____

Have you ever read the whole Bible?

_____

Would you consider doing it?

_____

You can google Daily reading plans for scripture and read it or listen to it. Or google free Bible to get a free copy.

Is there a friend you might ask to join you as an accountability partner?

_____

Has _____ ever read the Bible or become familiar with scripture?

_____

Would they accept a personal Bible from you? Or a New Testament?

_____

How do you sense God's presence?

_____

_____

_____

Have you sensed it this week? How?

_____

_____

_____

_____

Have you sensed any small change in _____ in relation to their spiritual openness? Not that it would be expected, but just be on the watch.

_____

_____

_____

Have you had any Divine Appointments lately? Something that just happened to work out where you felt God must have orchestrated it?

_____

_____

_____

How did they happen?

_____

_____

_____

Have you sensed any pushback?

_____

_____

_____

When you pray for another person, sometimes the blowback comes on you and you can find yourself facing hardship or discouragement yourself. It may seem to come out of the blue, with no warning and no logic to why things are happening. Praying for someone's salvation does not make the evil one happy. If this happens it's helpful to be sure you are praying on the Armor of God. If this is new to you, there's some instruction in the Appendix at the back of this book on pages 111–113.

Go back and read that part, and if you have not been, be sure that is part of your daily prayer. And pray for yourself, asking God to guard you and protect you, your family, your health, finances, relationships, home, job, and whatever else you feel led to pray about to keep you solid.

_____

_____

_____

_____

_____

_____

It also helps to talk with another Christian friend and ask them to pray for you and what you're experiencing. Or even for the duration of this commitment.

Conviction of Sin

Therefore, there is now no condemnation for those who are in Christ Jesus (Romans 8:1).

Heavenly Father, please reach _____ and convict their heart of their own personal sin. There could be lies they've told to cover wrong actions they've taken, maybe even illegal activity. Or sin could be attitudes that have been wrong, or words spoken out of anger or hate. Besides the Ten Commandments, You tell us that even choosing our own way over Yours is the sin of rebellion.

Aside from words spoken or actions taken, there are sins of omission, when _____ knew to do what was right but didn't do it. Let _____ see their sin for what it is and confess it to You as sin. That will lead them to Your forgiveness and redemption.

Conviction that comes from You lifts us up and inspires us to do better, to be better. It even motivates and empowers us to begin thinking and behaving in a different way. It draws us to You for forgiveness and cleansing (1 John 1:9). And it releases us from the penalty of that sin.

Father, lift _____. Inspire them to do better, to be better. Motivate and empower _____ to begin thinking and behaving in a different way. Draw _____ to You to confess their sin and ask for forgiveness and cleansing. Release them from the penalty of that sin and let them feel the freedom they have in You.

The opposite of Your conviction and forgiveness is how the devil uses our sin to condemn us. Do not let _____ feel that condemnation that would drag them down. This evil one would use it to ensnare them into defeat: guilt, shame, and hopelessness, and then use it to control them.

Father, even if _____ feels the sin You bring to their mind was in some way justified, or they have rationalized it in a way to remove their sense of responsibility or accountability or feel they have already paid for the sin themselves, bring them to the realization of their need to see it as You see it. And confess it. Amen

Desire to Turn From Evil

Flee the evil desires of youth and pursue righteousness, faith, love and peace (2 Timothy 2:22).

Turn from your evil ways. Observe my commands and decrees (2 Kings 17:13).

Heavenly Father, now that _____ has begun to recognize ungodly influences and sin, give them a desire to turn away from them. Whether these come from the world around them or from within their own flesh or from the evil one, do not let them lust after or want to participate in them any longer.

Psalm 1:1-2 says, *"Blessed is the one*
who does not walk in step with the wicked
or stand in the way that sinners take
or sit in the company of mockers,
but whose delight is in the law of the LORD,
and who meditates on his Law day and night."

Help _____ reject the advice of manipulative, ungodly people and not do what they do. Don't let them enjoy going along with a crowd who lives in sin. And let _____ clean up their language and thought life so they even cringe when hearing others mock You or take Your name in vain.

Father, these influences may come in the innocent looking guise of social values, politics, or even marketing strategies that seem to make sense for the times we live in. But the times are evil and so are the pressures that draw people in. Or the influences may be more easily recognizable as indulgences of the flesh, the curiosity of evil, or the outright deception of false religions.

Let whatever rewards those might seem to offer lose their luster. And grant _____ a sense of disgust and revulsion when they think of going along with the crowds that follow those paths. Help them see the benefits of changing their behavior, values and maybe even relationships.

Begin to show _____ a Biblical world view with the absolute moral truth of the Bible as their guide in making decisions and living their life. In this way, let _____ be blessed. Amen

Role Models

Follow my example, as I follow the example of Christ
(1 Corinthians 11:1).

Heavenly Father, please send godly role models into _____'s life. Bring people who will speak Your truth and model how to live that truth in this ungodly world.

In many ways we are past the point of them listening to me or following my example, but You know the kind of person that can impact and influence _____. Send someone they will respect and listen to into their sphere of contact who will make an impression on them.

Open _____'s eyes and ears to the presence of these role models. Create opportunities for them to interact. And let those experiences illustrate the differences between how _____ is choosing to live their life and the better way the role model is making decisions, believing, and behaving.

Father, give _____ a desire to change. Help _____ see the steps they need to take away from the things that pull them away from You and towards a godlier way to live. Reward even the tiniest step they take in Your direction. Amen.

Hunger and Thirst

Show me your ways, Lord, teach me your paths. Guide me in your truth and teach me, for you are God my Savior (Psalm 25:5).

Heavenly Father, give _____ a hunger and thirst for truth. Do not let them be satisfied any longer with the lies and deceptions fed to them by the world and the evil one. When they hear something false, make them aware of it immediately on a new level, in a new way that spurs them on to investigate and not simply take it at face value. Don't let _____ make any decision or choose a direction based on anything they haven't checked out for themselves.

Put resources in _____'s life to be able to get to the bottom, to the truth of whatever matters You direct them to. Whether it's a Bible, a website, or a person who can shed Your light on the matter, protect them from false resources, websites or people who would misdirect them and lead them away from the truth.

Give _____ a hunger and thirst to know Your Word, the Bible. When they hear verses of scripture, or stories from the Bible, or even remember something they already know of scripture, give them a new sense of understanding of what it really means and how to apply it to their life. And let that feed a desire to know more.

Give them a hunger and thirst for Your will in their lives so that nothing will hinder them from coming to You. Let this be a lifelong appetite for You and the truth. Amen

PART 3

Show Them You Care

Unique Identity

I praise you because I am fearfully and wonderfully made; your works are wonderful. I know that full well (Psalm 139:14).

Heavenly Father, give _____ an awareness of the unique way You have created them. Let them begin to see the special personality, talents, and experiences that have affected who they are today.

Rather than be dissatisfied with how they look or what talents they have or don't have, let _____ begin to see themself through Your eyes, from Your perspective. And let that be the source of their sense of value and worth.

Empower _____ with a true sense of identity, made in Your image, not defined by a job or role that carries responsibilities and expectations that determine their value based on how well they perform.

Father, reveal to _____ and let them begin to see that they are:
>*chosen by You, holy and dearly loved,*
>*Your child,*
>*Your workmanship,*
>*fearfully and wonderfully made,*
>and the beloved who You *rejoice over with singing*! Amen

Daily Bread

Give me neither poverty nor riches, but give me only my daily bread (Proverbs 30:8).

Heavenly Father, You have taught us to ask for our "daily bread" in The Lord's Prayer. I am asking for You to provide for _____'s daily bread. If _____ has more than they need, they will think they are providing for themselves and don't need You. If they have too little, they can become angry, bitter, and turn away from You, perhaps even turn down a dark path to get what they need.

Father, more than simply food, I am asking for You to grant _____ whatever it is they need to get through today. Be there, close to them, providing whatever the need of the moment calls for. It blows my mind that You, the Creator of the universe, are mindful of every need of every individual You have created—every person on the entire planet! Those needs change every day, sometimes every hour.

I trust You to see to _____'s practical, relational, mental, emotional and spiritual needs as well. _____ may not even realize what those needs are, but You know. And when You meet those needs and provide what is necessary, let them see You are the one graciously providing for and sustaining them.

I acknowledge that their very life is a gift from You, Father. Every breath they take, every beat of their heart is only by Your grace. I am so grateful that _____ is in my life. Thank You for meeting their needs. Amen

Be Their Shepherd—Psalm 23

The Lord is my shepherd, I lack nothing (Psalm 23:1).

Heavenly Father, You are the Good Shepherd. Please go after this sheep, _____, who has wandered away from You. They have become entangled in the thorny briars of this world and have lost their way. _____ no longer hears Your voice to guide them into green pastures and away from swift-moving deep waters that can drown them.

_____ has been taken by another shepherd, one who is not good, who does not look out for, care for, and protect his sheep. One who would sell this sheep's very life for profit. Father, deliver _____ from this evil.

Restore _____'s soul as only You can. Draw them out of their wayward behaviors and beliefs with Your staff. Lead _____ into paths of righteousness for Your name's sake. Even though _____ is walking in the shadow of death, they don't know it. Be with them. Comfort and protect them. Lead _____ back into Your flock where they can live in safety under Your tender care, forever. Amen

Reflections

Amazing job! You have completed Day 28!!

If you have not been able to be consistent in praying this week, what has gotten in your way?

_____

_____

_____

How can you remedy that?

_____

_____

_____

If you have missed any days, go back, and pray any prayers you missed. Take extra days if you need to.

_____

_____

_____

During your prayer time, has God showed you anything this week about Himself? About the one you're praying for?
About yourself?

_____

_____

_____

_____

_____

_____

In thinking back over the prayers prayed this week...

Who have been your role models in your spiritual life?

_____

_____

What have you learned from them?

_____

_____

_____

How do you see your unique identity in Christ?

What are some of the gifts, talents and experiences that make up who you are?

_____

_____

_____

How are you using those in positive ways?

_____

_____

_____

How do you see God as your Shepherd?

_____

_____

_____

A wonderful book that lends a deeper understanding of sheep and shepherds that was written by a shepherd, is *A Shepherd Looks at Psalm 23* by W. Phillip Keller

Heal Broken Places

"But I will restore you to health and heal your wounds,"
declares the Lord (Jeremiah 30:17).

Heavenly Father, move into any places _____ has brokenness, (Jeremiah 30:17a). Those places in their life where _____ is no longer strong physically, mentally, emotionally, or spiritually. Wherever there are broken places, speak Your life and Your healing. Give _____ faith to trust what You say: that You love them and that Your love is greater than whatever difficulty they're going through.

Heal those places where Christians have disappointed _____, let them down, even caused them pain. Let them separate the pain of being hurt by fallible humans and things that happened in churches, from their feelings and understanding of who You are.

These broken places are like weaknesses where they are vulnerable to temptation into sin and believing a lie. While You are healing those areas, protect and encourage _____. Protect them by hedging them in in front and back, along their sides, above and below so that no evil power can get in and lead them farther away from You. Encourage them by bringing someone alongside them to be wise counsel by checking their attitudes and guiding them in godly decisions. And who will strengthen them as they are healing.

Especially during these 40 days of prayer, be their strength and spread Your protection over _____'s body, mind and spirit. Watch over their physical health so no illness sidelines them. Meet their emotional needs where relationships have been broken by betrayal, unmet expectations, or dishonesty. Heal any spiritual wounds where they have been believing lies that kept them away from Your perfect love and salvation. Thank You for being their Healer: Jehovah Rophe. Amen

Hearing God

For he is our God and we are the people of his pasture, the flock under his care. Today, if only you would hear his voice (Psalm 95:7-8).

Whether you turn to the right or to the left, your ears will hear a voice behind you, saying, "This is the way; walk in it" (Isaiah 30:21).

Heavenly Father, let _____ hear Your voice. Maybe not audibly, but in whatever way You choose to reach out and communicate with them. Just like a radio receiver must be tuned in to a broadcasting frequency to hear the station broadcasting, teach _____ how to "tune" their spirit to hear You speak: be it from the Bible, in prayer, from sermons or podcasts, from other people, by observing nature, through their circumstances, in dreams or visions, from joys or even pain.

Sometimes the noise of the world drowns out the sound of Your voice. Show _____ how to be still and listen for it. Sometimes their own thoughts, the negative talk, self-doubt, and self-criticism can make Your message hard to hear. Teach _____ how to clear their mind to understand what You have to say. And sometimes sin can cause an "ear" infection that needs to be "cleaned out" confessed, for proper hearing.

As time goes by, I pray that _____ will learn to recognize Your voice. But today, help them make time to seek it. Let them know when they hear from You that it is indeed You, and how to confirm that. More than that. Give _____ an understanding of what You are saying to them.

Make it clear to _____ how You are leading them. You have given _____ ears to hear, let them hear, (Mark 4:9). Amen

Redeem What was Meant for Evil

You intended to harm me, but God intended it for good
(Genesis 50:20).

May the Lord answer you when you are in distress; may the name of the God of Jacob protect you (Joel 2:25 Psalm 20:1).

Heavenly Father, I bring _____ before You for Your blessing. They have experienced so many detrimental things. Some were brought on by unfortunate decisions, or just being in the wrong place at the wrong time. Whatever those circumstances brought, show something positive from them: a lesson learned, a contact made, a changed perspective.

And in some ways, these detrimental experiences were brought on by the devil leading them astray. Lord, show _____ that You can take even what the evil one has meant for their harm and redeem it into something good. Do not let the devil get a foothold in their life, their mind or their spirit by the harm that has been caused. But instead, use every experience and make something good from it. Do not let anything they have gone through be wasted.

Many times, the hardest things we experience become touchpoints to connect with other people who can help us or who we can help. And sometimes the most difficult issues we deal with bring out weaknesses in us that cut through our pride and ignorance to bring us to the place where we turn to You. Connect _____ with someone who can help them or who they can help.

Father, use it all for good in _____'s life. Amen

Bless—Psalm 20

May the Lord answer you when you are in distress; may the name of the God of Jacob protect you. May he send you help from the sanctuary and grant you support from Zion. May he give you the desire of your heart and make all your plans succeed (Psalm 20:1-2,4).

Heavenly Father, use my words to bless _____. Train me in the ability to speak the truth in love. Set a watch over my mouth to stop unthinking and hurtful words before they are spoken, and damage is done.

One way to bless _____ is to use Your very words. Today I use these words from Psalm 20, inserting _____'s name:

"O Lord, answer _____ when he is in distress;" (place in their heart the desire to call out to You and let them hear Your voice above all else going on in their life), *"may the name of the God of Jacob protect _____."* (Protect their life, their health, their relationships, their mind, their emotions, their spirit, their work, their comings, their goings)

"May You send _____ help from Your sanctuary" (where You sit enthroned and have angels to be Your messengers and do Your bidding) *"and grant him support from Zion."*

"Would You give _____ the desire of their heart" (and remove any desires that would take them away from You) *"and make all their plans succeed."* (As You direct their steps)

"We will shout for joy when _____ is victorious and will lift up our banners in the name of our God!" Amen!

Use Circumstances

When he [the Prodigal son] came to his senses...he got up and went to his father. But while he was still a long way off, his father saw him and was filled with compassion for him; he ran to his son, threw his arms around him and kissed him (Luke 15:17, 20).

Heavenly Father, please use the circumstances in _____'s life to draw them to You. Call their attention to the big broad strokes they paint their life with and the tiny brush strokes that make up the details. It could be the big events or even the smaller, everyday routine occurrences.

If there is joy in their life, let them see that it is not just good luck or their own efforts that have brought the joy. Let them see beyond the circumstance or seeming coincidence to the power behind the blessing that came from You.

If there are difficult conditions, or even tragic sorrows, do not let those be wasted. Regardless of what brought them on: their own bad decisions, the work and influence of the evil one, or mere happenstance; use those to get their attention. Like the Prodigal son in the pigsty (Luke 15:11-32), let _____'s circumstances confront them in a way that can't be ignored. Don't let any turmoil they have gone through lead them down a dark path. But use it to bring _____ to a saving knowledge of You.

Father, I would love to see _____ drawn to You by blessing and joy. But understand that even with us, sometimes You must use other measures to get our attention. Please do whatever it takes to bring them to You to hear and accept Your invitation for a blessed eternity. Amen

Mentors

*You, however, know all about my teaching, my way of life,
my purpose, faith, patience, love, endurance...But as for you,
continue in what you have learned and have become convinced
of, because you know those from whom you learned it*
(2 Timothy 3:10, 14).

Heavenly Father, besides just people in _____'s life who model godly living, bring someone into their life who will take an active interest in them and in their spiritual development. It may be someone they already know. Or it could be a brand-new contact who they can make a connection with.

Let there be opportunities for _____ and this mentor to have protected conversations about spiritual issues. Let this mentor be a teacher, a guide, a person who by being connected to You, can show _____ Your light, and the way they need to go.

Give this mentor opportunities to observe and speak into _____'s life on all kinds of issues: relational, work, financial, social and spiritual. Give them Your wisdom to know how to interact with and be involved with _____ in a natural, relaxed way.

Thank You that You use ordinary people in all our lives for extraordinary purposes. And thank You that even though my own influence may be waning, You are well-prepared with others to come into _____'s life. Amen

Deliverance

*For the LORD your God is the one who goes with you
to fight for you against your enemies to give you victory*
(Deuteronomy 20:4).

Heavenly Father, I am asking that You would provide _____ with a supernatural deliverance in one area in their life where they've been struggling. I could probably name some things, but You know the biggest thing in their life that keeps them from coming to you.

Give them an immediate victory—loosen the bonds of whatever has kept them away from salvation. If _____ has been bound or chained with an addiction or worshiping an idol or some other power in their life, break those chains. Or if there is some behavior they've been trying to control or stop, remove the desire and the urgency to continue in it.

Father give _____ an immediate release and open their eyes so they can see Your power personally at work in their own life right now! And replace it with a realization that You have blessed them with this freedom they have from their old ways.

If this behavior or wrong belief has taken _____ far from You, show them the way back to You. If they must cover a lot of ground to come to you, encourage them along the way. Guide their steps and protect them from being waylaid by the world or the desires of their flesh or the evil one.

Draw _____ to You, Father. Deliver them from the grasp of idolatry or sin or evil. Give them a victory in a struggle that releases them to come to You for salvation. Amen

Reflections

You are almost there!!! Good for you!

If you have not been able to be consistent in praying this week, what has gotten in your way?

_____

_____

_____

How can you remedy that?

_____

_____

_____

_____

If you have missed any days, go back, and pray any prayers you missed. Take extra days if you need to.

During your prayer time, has God showed you anything this week about Himself? About the one you're praying for?

_____

_____

_____

_____

About yourself?

_____

_____

_____

In thinking back over the prayers prayed this week...

Are there specific broken places or experiences you know about in _____'s life that need special prayers for God's healing?

_____

_____

How have you heard God's voice?

_____

_____

_____

When God speaks, it's worth writing down, so you don't forget, and so you remember accurately how you are supposed to act on it.

Is there something in your life that God has worked out for good even though it was meant for evil?

_____

_____

_____

Can you think of a time when you experienced a hardship, and it drew you to God?

_____

_____

_____

Is there an area in _____'s life where you know they are struggling? Pray again for freedom from that specific struggle.

_____

_____

_____

Evil Armor

The thief comes only to steal and kill and destroy (John 10:10).

For he is a liar and the father of lies (John 8:44).

Heavenly Father, just as You come to give us abundant life, the evil one seeks to destroy, offering counterfeit armor. This may appear protective, but will destroy the one I pray for. If _____ has picked up any of this "evil armor," I ask for You to remove it from them now.

Remove the "helmet of destruction" that encourages sinful and destructive thought. While _____ may feel indestructible, this will cause damage to their relationships and future. _____ will be blind to consequences and act on ideas without discernment.

The evil "breastplate" is one of self-righteousness and self-entitlement. It creates a false sense of what is right, focusing only on what they feel they deserve or are owed, this will lead _____ to act in ways that will distance them from You and others who love them.

Take away the "belt of lies and deceit" that allows _____ to live by the morality of the times, doing what they feel is right for them, or whatever they can get away with. This "belt" will undermine _____'s relationships and destroy their life with a moral and spiritual debt they can never repay. Remove their "shoes" of disunity and strife that allow _____ to literally and figuratively walk all over people.

Don't let _____ hold up a "shield of intolerance" against anyone or anything that doesn't agree with their version of truth. Or knock down anyone with standards different from them.

And convince _____ to lay down "swords of idolatry." These idols are used to make decisions that _____ may think will bring them happiness and success. But from materialism to humanism to worshipping fame, wealth, power, beauty, comfort, or false religions, these idols are deceptive and keep people from seeking You. Those who wield them fight against anyone and any belief that would lead them to the One True God, You.

Father, all this false, counterfeit, "evil armor" makes it harder for _____ to see the truth. Piece by piece, strip it away so _____ can see You and see the truth for what it is. Amen

You Who began a Good Work

Being confident of this, that he who began a good work in you will carry it on to completion until the day of Christ Jesus (Philippians 1:6).

Heavenly Father, You have promised that for believers, *"He who began a good work in you will carry it on to completion until the day of Christ Jesus"* (Philippians 1:6). I believe You are calling _____. And that there is more to the work You desire to do in them through the Holy Spirit, beginning with their salvation.

I thank You Father that I can trust Your Word here because Your character is trustworthy. You are completely faithful in performing what You say You will do. Would You let the work of the Holy Spirit's calling _____ to salvation be just the beginning of all You will accomplish in and through _____'s life?

Remove any obstacle in their soul so they hear Your call. Let _____'s answer to Your call be the saving of their soul. And let that be just the first step in a life given over to You. I trust Your timing. And I understand that You do not experience time as humans do. With You *"a thousand years in Your sight is like a day,"* (Psalm 90:4). But I ask that You allow me to see Your hand at work in _____'s life and be blessed to see You continuing Your good work in them.

Thank You for being faithful and true. Thank You for Your patience with us. Amen

Temptation

And lead us not into temptation, but deliver us from the evil one (Matthew 6:13).

Heavenly Father, there are so many things in this world that are temptations. We are tempted to do things that are not good for us, for our bodies, our minds, or our spirits. We are also tempted to *not* do things that *are* good for our bodies, our minds, or our spirits.

You tell us we are tempted by our own desires, (James 1:14). But the world and the evil one have gotten good at exaggerating those passing thoughts and simple desires and elevating them by downplaying the negative effects or consequences and playing up the part that sounds good, or looks good, or will make us feel good.

Help _____ see past the worm on the hook to the devastation of being caught on the hook. Give them a supernatural awareness of the real consequences and negative outcomes from decisions they make or actions they take or don't take.

The next time _____ is tempted, show them the reality of the trap that has been set for them. Send the Holy Spirit to bring to their mind ways that they can avoid and turn away from that temptation before it leads them where they don't want to go. And reward them when they do turn from it. Then let that become the normal habit of behavior for _____ as they realize and find the blessing in doing good. Amen

Establish

So is my word that goes out from my mouth: It will not return to me empty, but will accomplish what I desire and achieve the purpose for which I sent it (Isaiah 55:11).

Heavenly Father, establish a lasting work in _____'s life. Let Your Word and influence spread like wildfire in their thoughts and attitudes and actions. I believe Your Word will not return void, and as I have prayed Your Word over _____ I am trusting that it will continue to bear fruit long after these 40 days have passed.

Draw _____ to You in big ways and in small ones. Reward even the tiniest steps they take in Your direction. Bless them in ways they have never even dreamed of. And let it be plain in their minds and spirits that these blessings have come from You, without a doubt.

In the words of Isaiah 11:2-3, may the Spirit of the Lord rest on _____.

The Spirit of wisdom and understanding.

The Spirit of counsel and might.

The Spirit of the knowledge and fear of the Lord.

May _____ delight him/herself in the fear of the Lord.

May _____ never ever forget that You are with them and that they are Your child. May that remembrance be a powerful deterrent and an awesome reassurance. Amen

Aaronic Blessing

*"The L*ORD* bless you and keep you; the L*ORD* make his face shine on you and be gracious to you; the L*ORD* turn his face toward you and give you peace"* (Numbers 6:24-26).

Lord Jesus Christ, As Aaron, the High Priest, gave this blessing over the people of Israel, I pray it now over _____. Defining the six Hebrew verbs adds a deeper understanding of the blessing's meaning:

May You, Lord God, the Holy One, infuse _____ with unlimited potential and power and release them from any restrictions or limitations that would prevent them from reaching the fullness of their potential to participate in their divine purpose which You have given them.

May You zealously cherish and treasure _____, diligently defending and keeping watch over them to protect and save them.

May the light of Your innermost being and essence illuminate _____ physiologically and spiritually, impacting their body, mind, soul, and spirit with Your warming, healing, soothing, restorative, empowering, and constantly renewing energy.

May You, the Holy One, give _____ what they really need, not out of pity, benevolence, generosity, or some misguided thought that they have earned it, but because You have promised, as the stronger covenant partner, to strengthen them and enable them to reach their potential and enjoy the covenant You entered into with them, when they accepted You as Savior.

As You were in the Holy of Holies, may You be present with _____ so they can experience true spiritual reality.

And may You place in and establish in _____ wholeness, wellness, purposeful living in joy, with abundant provision, harmony, safety, and security summed up in the Hebrew word "Shalom."

This expanded definition of the six Hebrew verbs in the Aaronic blessing comes from *Bill Bullock, The Rabbi's Son.*[1]

---

1. Bullock, Bill. 2009. "Torah Naso: Numbers 6:24-27." Torah Study Written Archives. https://biblicallifestylecenter.org/uploads/bill/pdfs/Naso/5781/35Chamishi81.pdf

The "Priestly Blessing"

Y'varechecha Adonai
[May the Holy One bless you]

v'yish'merecha
[and zealously cherish and keep watch over you]

Ya'er Adonai panav elecha
[May the Holy One's Face shine upon you]

v'chuneka
[and shower you with grace]

Yisa Adonai panav elecha
[May the Holy One lift up His countenance upon you]

v'yasem lecha shalom
[and may He give you wholeness, wellness, security, abundant provision, and peace].
[Numbers 6:24-26]

Reflections

CONGRATULATIONS!! You made it!!

You finished the work you started! You did it! The whole 40 days!

We are so proud of you!!

How does it feel?

_____

_____

_____

During your 40 day prayer journey, has God shown you anything new about Himself?

_____

_____

_____

How will you apply that to your life?

_____

_____

_____

_____

Have you learned anything about the one you prayed for?

_____

_____

_____

Will that change the way you think about them or interact with them?

_____

_____

_____

_____

Has God shown you anything new about yourself?

_____

_____

_____

_____

Do you feel any differently about prayer? The way God works in others? In you?

_____

_____

_____

_____

_____

_____

Is there someone else's salvation you can pray for now?

_____

_____

_____

_____

AFTERWARDS

Thank You After 40 Days

Heavenly Father, thank You for letting me pray intentionally and consistently for this individual these 40 days. I pray that through these prayers Your power will be released on _____ that will bring them to a saving knowledge of You.

I continue to pray that You will make Your presence known in their life. That _____ will sense the call of the Holy Spirit into a saving relationship with You that will change their life now and for all eternity. I continue to thank You and call on You to affect Your will and Your purpose in their life. Joining my prayer with Your purpose that none should perish but all have everlasting life. Amen

When They Are Saved—Confirmation

Heavenly Father when _____ turns to You, confirm in their life that there has been a spiritual change in them. Give them some accompanying supernatural sense that verifies the realization of what has happened. Something that they know that they know that they know. Something that is different now because they have a place in Your kingdom, and an eternal home with You.

Give _____ a new perspective or a new outlook on how they see the world, a sure realization that they are no longer blinded or deafened by the overt and subtle influences of the world. Assure _____ that their spiritual eyes and ears have been opened to see and hear truth and to acknowledge it as truth.

Give them a desire, a hunger to go after and seek truth, pushing aside what they used to believe that got in the way of them coming to you. Let it affect their relationships, their work, their sense of purpose in the world. Let this confirmation affect the way they eat and drink and sleep and talk and joke and socialize and worship.

And we will all rejoice! Giving You the glory and thanks and praise for bringing _____ to a saving relationship with You! Amen!

Appendix

Not sure what to say if salvation conversations come up? No problem, we've got you covered. Have a look at the resources that follow, to use in your own life, and those you're praying for.

Guide to Salvation Prayer

So, the person you've been praying for has suddenly called you up, dropped all pretense, and is now asking you what they need to do next. They're ready to surrender their life to Christ.

Sweet! You've done all the hard work, praying for them each day. This next part is simplicity itself.

Admit, Confess, Repent, Trust.

You admit that Jesus is who He says He is in the Bible, that you need His help and will turn from how you've been living and instead choose to follow Him in this life each day from now on. That's pretty much it.

Ask Him to come into your life, wipe out the sin that separates you from God, and then thank him for making it all happen. Done. Now celebrate!

Rather have the 'read through' version you're now used to? No problem. Read and pray this together and you're all set, except for the celebration hugs.

Father, it is written in Your Word that if I confess with my mouth that Jesus is Lord and believe in my heart that You have raised Him from the dead, I shall be saved.

Therefore, Father, I confess that Jesus is my Lord. I make Him Lord of my life right now. I believe in my heart that You raised Jesus from the dead. I turn from my past life and decisions and choose to follow You from now on.

I thank You for forgiving me of all my sin. Jesus is my Lord, and I am a new creation. Old things have passed away; now all things become new in Jesus' name. Amen

APPENDIX B

Who You Are in Christ Now

What happens the split second after you choose to trust in God? When you choose to become a believer in Jesus Christ, you are changed in ways you and I cannot imagine. In an instant, who you are and what's true of you have all completely changed.

Take time to review the list of just some of these changes below. Check out the verse references for any that you find particularly hard to trust or believe.

I am chosen of God, holy and dearly loved. Col 3:12
I am chosen and dearly loved by Christ to bear his fruit. John 15:16
I am the salt of the earth. Matt 5:13
I am a child of God. John 1:12
I am a daughter/son of light and not darkness. I Thess 5:5
I have been made righteous. 2 Cor 5:21
I am free forever from condemnation. Rom 8:1
I am united to the LORD and am one spirit with him. I Cor 6:17
I am a member of Christ's body. I Cor 12:27, Eph 5:30
I am a holy partaker of a heavenly calling. Heb 3:1
I have been redeemed and forgiven, and I am the recipient of his lavish
    grace. I have been made alive together with Christ. Eph 2:5
I may approach God with boldness, freedom, and confidence. Eph 3:12
I have been redeemed and forgiven of all my sins. The debt against me has
    been cancelled. Col 1:14
Christ Himself is in me. Col 1:27
I have been made complete in Christ. Col 2:10
I have been given the spirit of power, love and a sound mind. 2 Tim 1:7
I am God's handiwork, created in Christ Jesus to do the work which He has
    prepared in advance for me. Eph 2:10
I am born of God, and the evil one, the devil, cannot touch me. 1 John 5:18

There will be a lot of voices speaking into your new way of life. Old friends, new friends, family members and more. Even your own internal "negative self-talk" might start to sound different to you now.

Did any of the truths above sound like something you've "heard" said is *not* true of you? From your friends? Inside your own head, maybe? Saying—it couldn't possibly be true of you. No way—and yet? Maybe take a moment to review those specific truth claims again.

Even better, write out those verses on sticky notes and put them in places where you will be sure to see each one in the coming days, weeks, and months. You're running a race now, and you don't want to get distracted by conflicting opinions and veer out of your lane.

Your life in Christ is just beginning. The evil one is not pleased, but too bad. You belong to Christ now, and everything is about to get amazing!

"But you are a chosen people, a royal priesthood, a holy nation, God's special possession, that you may declare the praises of him who called you out of darkness into his wonderful light" (1 Peter 2:9).

APPENDIX C

So how do I know for sure that I've been saved?

I've heard of all kinds of experiences people have when they are "saved." If mine is different, or not as flashy, or emotional, or full of "spiritual fireworks," is it still just as real? What if it's just a quiet trust that brings a smile to my face alone?

How do I know for sure I've been Saved?

No worries, and yes, you are right to assume that as all people are different, all salvation experiences will be different too. Some people list a quiet cup of coffee as their happy place. Some paint their bodies and jump around at sporting events. Some people laugh out loud. Often. Some are content to know they made the right choice and that is satisfaction enough.

Beyond the personal experience, there are some age old tried-and-true ways to know your salvation is for real.

1. Trust in your salvation the same as you trusted in Christ for it.

If you believe the truths in the Bible by faith, you can also trust in your new salvation with that same faith. And the Bible is clear, if you've trusted in Christ, it's a done deal. There is no going back to where you once were. It's you and Jesus from here on out.

"For I am convinced that neither death nor life, neither angels nor demons, neither the present nor the future, nor any powers, neither height nor depth, nor anything else in all creation, will be able to separate us from the love of God that is in Christ Jesus our Lord," Romans 8:38-39.

2. Feelings, sort of, but not quite.

Feelings fade, and can be downright deceitful at times, but in the short term, they can also be a wonderful confirmation. The joy, the peace, the enthusiasm for what you've just done is all very real. Will it last? Not at all. But that's why we base our faith on Christ, the unchanging anchor for how we think, act, and feel about the world we live in. All else fades or disappoints, including our feelings, but Christ alone is unchanging God.

"Jesus Christ is the same yesterday and today and forever"(Hebrews 13:8).

3. Look for the fruit.

Paul mentions it, the Bible describes it, and you'll be seeing it in yourself soon enough. Your temper may decrease, or you may be less jumpy, less inclined to fight with your spouse, sibling, or boss. Maybe it's a peace where there shouldn't be. A calm sense of God working things out even when life is crazy and those around you are losing their heads.

That's the fruit of the Holy Spirit. Showing up in you and me as we live out our lives, trying to follow His guidelines for righteous living. Like watering a tiny tree, eventually it blossoms and bears fruit that you, and those around you all notice.

Be patient. Be kind. Don't lie or cheat. Believe the best in others. Support and encourage them. Love them like you'd want to be loved. The guidelines are simple, and the payoff just helps make even more happen.

Give it a try. Ask Jesus to help you out; see how you can relate to the world around you differently, starting today. *

"Whoever has the Son has life; whoever does not have the Son of God does not have life. I write these things to you who believe in the name of the Son of God so that you may know that you have eternal life" (1 John 5:12-13).

*Feel more than free to snap these pages with your phone and send them to the person you were praying for!

APPENDIX D

What do I do next?

The believer's life can be tricky at the very first. Before you set down roots, our enemy will look to distract or minimize the Truth and its impact on you. Have a look at how Jesus Himself described it:

"Listen then to what the parable of the sower means: When anyone hears the message about the kingdom and does not understand it, the evil one comes and snatches away what was sown in their heart. This is the seed sown along the path. The seed falling on rocky ground refers to someone who hears the word and at once receives it with joy. But since they have no root, they last only a short time. When trouble or persecution comes because of the word, they quickly fall away. The seed falling among the thorns refers to someone who hears the word, but the worries of this life and the deceitfulness of wealth choke the word, making it unfruitful. But the seed falling on good soil refers to someone who hears the word and understands it. This is the one who produces a crop, yielding a hundred, sixty or thirty times what was sown" (Matthew 13:18-23).

How do we keep this from happening? How do you as a new believer keep the flame alive, fanning it into a fire that will never go out, bringing warmth and light to others? Here are some time-tested methods for any Christian to engage in and keep the Word alive in them.

Daily prayer.

Our Lord God loves prayer. He loves hearing you bring Him into your life, sharing the ups and downs. What makes you anxious? What would help you in your Christian walk, just for today? Sharing these things with God in prayer, each day, throughout your week is one of the very best ways to grow and strengthen your relationship with Him.

Daily time in God's Word, the Bible.

Choose your version, NIV, ESV, maybe old-school King James, or even a paraphrase like The Message, but whatever makes God's Word accessible and understandable to you, that's where you want to be. Learning about God. Learning His guidelines for living. Hearing stories of Old and New Testament believers and seeing how they lived out their faith.

Having Jesus' life to emulate, and other followers of Christ to learn from, it all adds up. Just invest time every day to expose yourself to His supernatural Word.

Get a Devotional.

Buy one or find something free online. Whatever works, because sure, you can flip through the Bible and read whatever comes up, but you're probably going to find more applicable knowledge for day-to-day living in Paul's letters to the early church than in Old Testament lists of how to handle mold. A devotional book will bounce you around the Bible, highlighting stories of the kings of old, stories of warriors and prophets stepping out in faith. The miracles of God from Creation to the Red Sea; resurrecting his followers and making the sun stand still. Devotionals get you into books of the Bible you might not come across for months, showing you the highlight reel of God's Word.

Not sure about which Devotional book to try? Have a look at some we offer at the back of this book!

Connect with other believers.

Find a Bible-believing church of fellow believers and start to attend regularly. Like a waterfall in a dry and dusty land, coming together with others will strengthen you, encourage you, build you up, and bring you into relationships with fellow believers, as well as with opportunities to serve and praise God together.

Whether it's the teaching, the singing, or sharing with others, all of it helps you grow and become stronger in your faith walk.

Remember, there are lots of people who say they are Christians but might not be following Jesus exactly. Paul had them in Bible times, and we still have them today. They might mean well, but it's gotten to be more about the rules than relationship with Christ. You'll know these groups pretty easily if you look for two things:

1. If they make a big deal about Jesus, good. If they make a bigger deal about "dress this way, talk this way, don't drink, don't smoke, don't swear" and all the other rules, then keep an eye out.

2. Remember who Jesus got along with during his time on earth. The outcasts. The losers. Who did He *not* connect with? The religious authorities. Oops. Just remember with any group, no matter how religious, make a note of how they react if you *break the rules*. Offering grace and helping you back up? Good deal. If they get mad, very mad? Probably okay to look for a different church family, sorry.

There are some not-so-good things about the church at times. Even worse? If I'm not careful I start to be part of it myself...Ugh. But hey, we all fall, and that's why we look for God's loving, restoring grace. To get back up and start sharing His love with our world again.

And that's pretty much it. Giving up your old bad habits? That's up to you and Jesus. Should you dress differently? Read different stuff or change the way you talk?

Maybe for these first few weeks, just be you. Relax. Spend time in prayer, learn all you can about God, and start living out what you read, a little more each day.

Listening to Christian music, reading only Christian books, and dressing in church clothes every day is entirely up to you.

Confession and Repentance

Let God speak to you now and show you any sin you need to confess. Psalm 66:18 tells us if we cherish sin in our hearts, God won't listen to our prayers.

But 1 John 1:9-10 tells us, *"If we confess our sins, he is faithful and just and will forgive us our sins and purify us from all unrighteousness. If we claim we have not sinned, we make him out to be a liar and his word is not in us."*

Ask God if there are sins of:

THOUGHT—impure, selfish, angry, fearful, jealous

ATTITUDE—prideful, judgmental, argumentative, lukewarm toward God

SPEECH—crude, inappropriate, grumbling, divisive, lies, half-truths

RELATIONSHIP—wrong or improper, physically, or emotionally
Do you need to forgive someone? Do you need to ask for forgiveness?
As a husband: are you providing spiritual leadership, guiding and nurturing your wife?
As a wife: are you honoring and respecting your husband?
As parents: are you modeling godly behavior and attitudes and teaching your children in love?
As children or teens: are you respectful and obedient?

COMMISSION—things that you have done, actions you have taken
Have you done something you know is wrong?
Do you guard your eyes?
Have you exposed yourself to the occult?
Do you have habits that are harmful to your body—mind—spirit?

OMISSION—things you have failed to do
Has God prompted you to do something you haven't?
Have you failed to do good when you could have?

SELF-RULE—rebellion, going your own way

    Are you following God or going your own way?

    Are you avoiding something He's told you to do?

    Or are you still doing something He's told you not to?

Spiritual Armor for Battle

"Finally, be strong in the Lord and in his mighty power. Put on the full armor of God, so that you can take your stand against the devil's schemes. For our struggle is not against flesh and blood, but against the rulers, against the authorities, against the powers of this dark world and against the spiritual forces of evil in the heavenly realms. Therefore, put on the full armor of God, so that when the day of evil comes, you may be able to stand your ground, and after you have done everything, to stand. Stand firm then, with the belt of truth buckled around your waist, with the breastplate of righteousness in place, and with your feet fitted with the readiness that comes from the gospel of peace. In addition to all this, take up the shield of faith, with which you can extinguish all the flaming arrows of the evil one. Take the helmet of salvation and the sword of the Spirit, which is the word of God.

And pray in the Spirit on all occasions with all kinds of prayers and requests. With this in mind, be alert and always keep on praying for all the Lord's people" (Ephesians 6:10-18)

We dress ourselves in the armor that Paul describes here. He wrote his letter to the Ephesians while he was in Rome, under house arrest, guarded by Roman soldiers. Every day, he saw men dressed in armor, bearing the insignia of their authority. The Holy Spirit must have inspired his analogy of a Christian "soldier."

Praying on the armor can be as simple as listing each piece and stating that you are putting it on and wearing it.

When we are praying for someone, or even ourselves, the devil doesn't like it. And even with his limited power here on earth, we can find ourselves under attack in ways that can lead us to feel discouraged, defeated, even want to give up.

But we rely on the fact that God's armor is the very best!

The **Belt of Truth** is a wide, tight band around the waist that holds pieces of the armor on as well as the sword. When we are wearing truth, we can more easily recognize the lies the devil would tempt us to believe. We will not be mesmerized by half-truths or deceptions.

The **Breastplate of Righteousness** protects our heart and vital organs, a kind of forerunner of the bulletproof vest. It stops and deflects stabs and projectiles. Our righteousness comes from Jesus Christ. His blood paid the price for our sin, and we gain the righteousness of the perfect life He lived. In that righteousness the devil cannot hold anything against us.

The **Shoes of the Gospel of Peace** will help us walk in the Spirit. Putting on shoes is a sign of readiness and preparedness. With these we are ready to carry the Good News of salvation and peace into our relationships and whatever challenges we face. With our feet protected like this we will have traction even when we feel unsteady and will be able to stand firm.

The **Shield of Faith** is not some puny little garbage can lid with a handle, but a head-to-toe protection, repelling the enemy's offensive weapons. When the shield was anointed with oil it would reflect the glare of the sun and blind the enemy. This shield covered a soldier from top to bottom, side to side and can join with others to form a wall of protection that will fend off an attacker while advancing in the field of battle.

Our faith in God protects us when the world or others tells us things are hopeless or cannot work out because we have the One True God who is all-knowing and all-powerful. We trust in His love for us and know that He has a plan for us, to give us hope and a future with Him in eternity. Every time He keeps a promise, or delivers us from some trouble, or stands with us in hardship, it builds or faith - strengthens our shields! And when we stand beside other believers in their faith, we are protected even more!

The **Helmet of Salvation** protects our head and identifies who we fight for. This helmet also protects our minds and helps guard our thoughts. The enemy would want to fill our minds with thoughts of doubt, fear and insecurity. But when thoughts and emotional responses are stirred up, we can hold them up to the light of truth: scripture. God's Word is the truth that will combat all that would discourage us.

And the **Sword of the Spirit** is God's Word and strikes at the lies the devil would use to try and defeat us. We can use it to refute any lies the devil tries to get us to believe. We can pray it as part of our prayers. We can speak it out loud as an attack on the enemy. There is power in the Word of God.

Here is a sample prayer:

Heavenly Father, I come before you with thanks for the armor that You give me, which is the best. With the belt of truth fastened around my waist, I say that I will not believe the lies the devil would try to use to confuse me. Give me clarity and understanding. Help me see past what the world and others would tell me, to what you want to say to me.

I wear the helmet of salvation to guard my mind, and I take every thought captive to You. The breastplate of righteousness I place over my chest to protect my heart.

I wear the shoes of peace to say that I am ready to hear from You and to obey what You tell me to do.

I take up my shield to repel all the arguments the evil one would send against me. And I take up the sword, the Word of God, as a weapon to help me stand firm against the devil's schemes.

Thank you for hearing my prayer. Amen.

About the Authors

Eric Sprinkle is an Author, Speaker, and Adventurer with a passion for drawing disengaged men and women back into a life that's challenging, exhilarating, and eye-opening. Founder of "Adventure Experience", he has traveled around the world, taught swift-water rescue for the U.S. military, and now speaks on risk-taking and the joy of living 'a slightly more dangerous lifestyle'. The author of the exciting "Adventure Devos" devotional series, Eric calls the playground of Colorado Springs, Colorado home and shoots photos of ballerinas, dancing along the sides of sheer red rock cliffs for fun.

Check out his website here—AdventureExperience.net

And if you don't believe the part about ballerinas, fact check it with his Vlog here—www.youtube.com/AdventureExperience-TheSeries

Laura Shaffer: An Army Brat moving almost every year till college, Laura was delighted to discover that wherever she went, God was always there ahead of her. Even though the houses, and friends changed, there was always Sunday School and church where she learned that God was always with her. And she felt it.

Through the years she continued in her awareness of God's presence, especially working in the yard and taking nature walks in beautiful, colorful, Colorado. She writes to encourage people to lean into God and learn from Him in their daily life through nature, scripture, circumstances and prayer.

And now she wants to help you experience God's presence - equipping you to pray more intentionally and consistently, to empower your prayer life, and deepen your relationship with God.

Check out Laura's blog at www.DailyBiblePrayer.wordpress.com for scripture-based examples of her prayers anytime.

Need an Adventure Speaker for your next event or group meet-up?

Need someone to talk about
- Risk
- Challenge
- Dealing better with Fear

Eric would love to hang out with your group!

He's ready to unpack the question of whether our Lord God calls us to adventure, and even share some fun stories about prayer books too! All with heart pounding stories and gorgeous photos!

Check out AdventureExperience.net today and let's connect for an inspiring, challenging time together!

LOVE LAURA'S PRAYERS?

Looking for more from your
new prayer partner Laura?

You've got it!

Have a look here
for daily prayers,
inspiring blogs, and more!

Check out her prayer blog—
www.dailyBibleprayer.wordpress.com

For her devotion blog—
www.hearmorefromGod.wordpress.com

LIS†EN
UP!
Lean in & Learn
from the Lord™

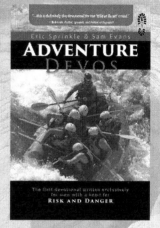

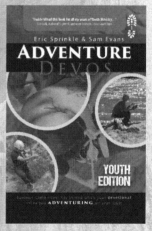

40DayPrayerGuides.com

Looking for another 40-Day Prayer Journey? Want to share and inspire others with stories from your last one? Welcome to the 40 Day Prayer Guide Series!

Be the first to download and check samples of the latest Guides, always weeks before they're listed for sale!

- Download free samples to share with friends
- Have a look at what's coming next in the 40-Day Prayer Guides series
- Share thoughts, ideas, and praises from your own 40-day journeys!

"This is a powerful book and is very much needed."

"I know several in my church right now who I plan to give copies to—real prayer warriors who would love this tool!"
(Early Reader Feedback)

Come have a look, sign up for the Newsletter and be more inspired in your prayer life today!